Put a Comma
After Love

poems by

Norma Ketzis Bernstock

Finishing Line Press
Georgetown, Kentucky

Put a Comma After Love

ACKNOWLEDGMENTS

The following poems have previously appeared, sometimes in a modified
version:

Adanna Fall, 2022. "Her Lover's Wife," "Is House Cleaning a Hostile Act?"
Caduceus Vol.2, 2004. "Her Lover Prefers the Snow"
Don't Write a Poem About Me After I'm Dead, Norma Ketzis Bernstock, 2011,
Big Table Publishing, "Endings"
Featured Poets Anthology, 2020. Moonstone Arts. "For Her Husband Who
Never Listened"
LIPS 42/43, 2015. "Disrepair"
MetaLand Poets of the Palisades II, 2016. "Cleaning House"
Paterson Literary Review, 2020. "Selling the House"
Poets' Invitational, August 2014. Grounds For Sculpture. "Courting"
Shattered Anthology, 2016. Kind of a Hurricane Press. "Urgent Care"

A big thank you to my dear friend, Douglas Adler, for the conversation that
produced the title of this chapbook.

Publisher: Leah Huete de Maines
Editor: Christen Kincaid
Cover Art: Tricia Adler
Author Photo: Fred Finck
Cover Design: Elizabeth Maines McCleavy

Order online: www.finishinglinepress.com
also available on amazon.com

Author inquiries and mail orders:
Finishing Line Press
PO Box 1626
Georgetown, Kentucky 40324
USA

Contents

Love Poem
Oh you…
What about me?
Nothing.
Everything.

Courting

(inspired by a sculpture of the same title by Seward Johnson)

She dangles a chip over his lips,
teasing,
his head in her lap, mouth open
anticipating the salty snack,
the sweet taste of her.
Where it begins…

She teases with hugs,
her scent, her pout.
I'll show you mine
if you'll show me yours.
Please, please me
and do you love me,
let's buy a house
and how many kids,
where to live,
how to live,
what couch to buy,
who pays the bills,
who cuts the grass,
let's entertain
and isn't this house a dream?

But whose dream
and whose life—
who's happy ever after?

Is House Cleaning a Hostile Act?

My mother, a reader not a writer, only had time
for Readers' Digest Condensed Books,
cleaned with a vengeance.
Brow scrunched, lips pursed,
red-faced she attacked—
purged memories of Europe's death camps,
swiped at cornered crumbs,
the difficult husband, hell-bent kids.

My sister loves order.
Collectible cups on a shelf
spaced two centimeters apart.
Her house is spotless, neat to a fault.
Beds made right after awakening
dare anyone to disturb the drape of the duvet.

My husband who never cleaned
always had time for himself.

To me he'd say:
    Ignore the dust.
He'd say:
    Let the dishes be.
He'd say:
    Don't bother with the beds.

I'd rage
then fling
his words
upon growing mounds of dirt.

I Never Owned a Pastry Blender

Never saw one in my mother's house,
a tool like the steel-blade chopper
she used with a wooden bowl—
chopped onions, celery and eggs.

I've chopped peppers and spices,
thrown in broken promises,
disappointments and despair.

Sometimes I'd blend them
together using a large spoon,
not a pastry blender
(if only I'd known).

I'd add a cup of salty tears,
boil the mess in a big pot,
delight in the rising steam
knowing that the mixture
would simmer and
reduce.

Endings

I heard that when a living thing dies
maggots consume the flesh.
My friend Paula told me this
after her rabbit died.

When my kitten died
I couldn't bare to part with her,
held her for hours
but worried that I'd see the maggots.

Finally my husband and I
entered the garden well after midnight,
he with flashlight and spade,
me hugging Mitzi tight in my arms.

I remember how we dug the grave,
buried her together
even though the two of us
were coming apart.

Chaos

The roller coaster ride
began with my father's death,
retirement and menopause
in the same year.
Clarity from hormonal shake-up
lead to divorce.
It was like the movie,
Shirley Valentine
in which a woman
travels to Greece,
leaves her husband behind
with stained kitchen counters
and thread-bare rugs.
I didn't go to Greece
but I did leave a husband
and a house with kitchen stains.
I took the rugs.

Selling the House

I left it up to my husband
to sell our house
after we divorced.
He'd been living there alone
for five years.

I left it up to him
to rid the house of those oversized
speakers he loved—
that blocked the picture window,
blocked the birch tree view.

It was his job
to sand and paint the back door
that rotted from neglect,
to add a railing on steps
my mother and his
could never climb,
up to him
to prune the azaleas and hedges
kept neat and trimmed by me.

I left it up to him
to fix the patio bricks,
patch the roof,
clean the gutters,
paint the shutters,
empty the attic
and basement boxes—
thirty years of accumulation.

It was my job to clear my head and heart—
his to sell the goddamn house!

For A Husband Who Never Listened

Her ex-husband continues
to give her gifts
after years apart
but not like the gifts from the past—
intimate lingerie he'd include
with every present
though she told him to stop,
told him she hated the push-up bras,
seamed stockings, crotchless panties
designed for whores,
her naked body never enough.

Today he stops by, says:
I have something for you,
a gift you'll like, he assures.

It's a crate of lumber, wood-stove size,
a gift that will burn and disappear
unlike the garter belts and thongs
that crowded dresser drawers
demanding:
Be the woman he wants.

In Search of

It began with a wire brush,
the one I couldn't find
but knew I owned,
could see in my mind
on a shelf in the garage
or in the toolbox drawer.

I searched the garage
and found a toilet seat
still in its box from
when the house was built,
three rubber pails
my boyfriend said to save—
he's gone about a year,
the pails remain.

I searched the pantry for
the brush, found a bag
of ornament hooks
(his), a menorah and skinny
colored candles (mine),
and dozens of phone cables
tangled in a box.

I cannot find the wire brush,
that hung on the pegboard hook
in the basement of
my marriage home.
I'll add it to the list
of all the things I've lost.

Finding a Former Boyfriend on Facebook

He's married, 50 years by now,
a snowbird between New York
and Delray Beach.
I've messaged him on Facebook—
Do you remember me?
but don't expect a response.

In his profile picture he's seated,
his blonde wife stands behind,
manicured fingers rest on his back.
His smile's changed, not the boyish
Sinatra-like grin that I loved.
Suddenly my cell phone beeps—it's him!
I imagine he's alone   free
to indulge in fantasy.

Remember the icy roads the night we parked,
your head on my chest,
the windows fogged over,
intense heat in the car?

I remember that wintry night,
the movie theater so packed
we sat in row one, how my neck ached
all night from staring up at the screen.

Who Needs Match.Com

Last night I feasted on pork medallions
with an Asian glaze, pickled salmon and
shrimp cocktail in a homemade sauce
prepared by a man who fancies himself a chef.
This man's not the one—
but he's the first since my break-up,
the first to share a bottle of wine,
kiss me good night, ask about my poems.

These days when I shop for hardware
at Home Depot, I hang around,
ask men questions about nuts and bolts
which gives me time to rate their assets—
more than a man who cooks,
I want a man who knows tools,
uses them skillfully
for renovation and repairs.

I watch how he handles
a sawblade, if he places it gently
on the rack, careful
with sharp edges
that can cut and hurt.

Her Lover Prefers the Snow

On this white December day
he pulls on fleece-lined boots,
slips into his orange slicker,
secures the snaps on the hood,
silently steals out the door.

In an hour's time
his face will resemble
the shade of sweet sherry.
Ice crystals like fragments
of cut glass
will cling to his beard.

But he, oblivious
to winter's chill,
will focus on the hemlocks
vested with frost,
how they bow low
revering nature's will.

White on white he calls
the veil of falling flakes.

Summoned by snow fields
dotted with fallen limbs,
crumbling barns
coated by windswept powder,
gelid landscapes that entice
this man away from
a woman who faithfully
feeds the fire and writes
about a lover
who sometimes
prefers the snow.

Lover

After Daughter by Lisel Mueller

My next poem will be happy,
I promise myself.
Then you appear
with your solid chest,
your receptive arms,
your love   your marriage.

All the sultry embraces,
the intimate night-long chats,
all the walks among lupine and Blues
        and this vibrant spring day
cannot change that.

Her Lover's Wife

She's envious
of her lover's wife
who shares a bed with him
whose body touches his
beneath the quilt
brushing backs
rubbing elbows, knees.

She's envious
of her lover's wife
who is the first
he sees in morning sun,
the last at night.
>*Who dreams* of daggers
>>*slipping*

Who sees him
shower and shave
pull on his slacks
straighten his tie
fill up his pockets
and empty them out.
>*Whose hollow dreams*
>>*echo in her head*

She's envious
of her lover's wife
who knows
the books he reads
the music that soothes
and songs he sings.
>*Who dreams of drumbeats*
>>*louder than her heart*

She's envious
of this woman
who is his wife
who is his wife

she is still his wife.

Urgent Care

I sit in the exam room
not at your house
where you, my new love
planned a dinner tonight,
salmon, green beans,
pie for dessert.

Instead you lay on your side,
bike shorts ripped,
skin broken and raw.
Road rash,
you said.

I didn't know then
when love was new
I'd be in other
hospitals with you.
But that was before,
before the biopsy,
CAT scans
and chemo infusions
when you would sleep
and I would write
to the rhythm of drugs
dripping through skin.

I remember I prayed
that I'd give you up
if that was the price
to pay for your life—

He lived.

Disrepair

I missed nothing
from the house I left.
Sunless rooms depressed me.
Tiny spaces that once seemed quaint
became too tight even for breath.
We never upgraded
the outdated fridge,
never fixed cracked bathroom tile—
clues to a marriage in distress.

He said it was hard leaving
his house after 20 years,
the dogs buried in the yard,
the vision of his daughter
sitting on the porch,
tennis racquet in hand,
he and his ex in the kitchen,
mixing sauce on the stove.

His kitchen cabinets no longer closed,
a missing bulb over the bathroom sink
never replaced, clues for sure.

He and I who found refuge
in each other's arms,
failed to see our own clues—
no spare bulbs in the closet,
a pantry begging for food.

My Boyfriend Explains a Peloton

Before I met my bike-racer boyfriend
I never heard of a peloton.
I learned the lingo as we watched
Le Tour and with patience
he explained.
Now I hold my own
conversing at post-race parties—

I can *budder* a chamois,
down a gel,
sync the meter.
I can clean cleats,
critique a crit,
cruise steady state,
sprint for interval training.

But what do I do
when bike-racer boyfriend
is no longer steady,
sprints for longer
and longer intervals,
drops me and races on?

In a world
of muscled quads,
sculpted calves
and superman glutes,
where is the heart?

Cleaning House

He's in her pantry,
in the jars of sauce,
the Old Bay Tin,
the mushroom cans.
He's in the fridge,
the second shelf,
the olive tapenade.
On the left,
the produce drawer,
blueberries and red.

She's cleaning house,
sweeping out,
removing signs of him—
the books he left,
socks and shorts,
slippers by the door,
the sateen sheets he loved so much,
he loved her on those sheets.
She'll wash and scrub and bleach them clean,
the sheets belong to her.
She'll sleep on sheets devoid of him,
on sheets   alone   untouched.

Ex

He left his Persian rug,
purple and red,
shades of blue   like his eyes.
Today I found his socks—
the ones in black
that matched my mood back then.

Does he miss these socks,
our pillow talks, my poems,
the house he built and named
the Tree House Home?
Its rooms with morning sun
through windowed walls,
the view of summer fiddle heads,
and autumn's golden splash.

These socks, too big,
will work for me—
a second layer over wool.
They'll warm my toes
through winter's ice and chill.

Starting Over

She bought several pairs of shoes today—
unprecedented.
She wanted a comfortable
stylish pair,
shoes that could go the distance,
help her navigate bumps in the road,
face challenging terrain,
shoes with support
for sharp turns
and steep descents.

To her surprise,
she found three
that fit the bill—
black oxfords with red laces,
gray slip-ons with a pink stripe
and patent leather heels
that remind her to walk tall
with grace and tenacity
no matter the landscape.

After retiring from a 34-year career in education as a middle school teacher, supervisor and media specialist in New York City and Northern New Jersey, **Norma Ketzis Bernstock** moved to Milford, Pennsylvania where she became a member of the Upper Delaware Writers Collective. She now works full-time writing and publishing her poetry which has appeared in many journals and anthologies including *Stillwater Review, Exit 13, Connecticut River Review, Paterson Literary Review, Lips, Rattle, Meta-Land—Poets of the Palisades II* and the *International Bilingual Anthology, Bridging the Waters, II.*

A first collection of poems appeared in her chapbook, *What We Remember*, the title poem about a father who suffers from dementia. Poet/journalist Charles Johnson writing in the Home News Tribune described her poetry as "…linguistically colorful…" referring to her poignant and entertaining narratives of family life, marriage and life after divorce. A second chapbook, *Don't Write a Poem About Me After I'm Dead*, was published by Big Table Publishing. Her poems have been featured online at *Your Daily Poem*, read on WJFF Catskill Radio, honored by the Paterson Poetry Center's Allen Ginsberg Awards and have received a Pushcart nomination.

Although writing is a priority, Norma enjoys creating photography-based art. Her images are used in collages, wall hangings and mixed media projects, including several that incorporate her poetry. She previously taught at several art associations in Northern New Jersey and is presently a member of arts alliances in the Catskill region of New York State and northeastern Pennsylvania.

www.ingramcontent.com/pod-product-compliance
Lightning Source LLC
Chambersburg PA
CBHW022109080426
42734CB00009B/1526